BYTE

THE AI REVOLUTION IN REAL ESTATE

SAM SINGH

USING
CHATGPT 4o

BYTE: THE AI REVOLUTION IN REAL ESTATE
SAM SINGH

ISBN: 9798335276801
IMPRINT: INDEPENDENTLY PUBLISHED

CONTENT

DEDICATIONS		i
PREFACE		iii
CHAPTER ONE	WHY AI? FIXING THE 98% PROBLEM	1
CHAPTER TWO	BUILDING BRIDGES OF TRUST *THE POWER OF AI AND PERFECT INFORMATION*	7
CHAPTER THREE	THE DEATH OF DIGITAL MARKETING *LASER-FOCUSED AI PROSPECTING IS THE FUTURE*	11
CHAPTER FOUR	DRIVING OFF-PLAN SALES *LEARNING TO FLY WITH AI*	17
CHAPTER FIVE	THE INCREDIBLE AI MIND READER *THE POWER OF HUMANISTIC TECHNOLOGY*	23
CHAPTER SIX	THE RISE OF THE MACHINES *AI-POWERED ROBOT SALES AGENTS*	31
CHAPTER SEVEN	THE FUTURE IS D2C *SELLING PROPERTY DEVELOPER 2 CONSUMER*	39
CHAPTER EIGHT	RISK, FEAR & ANXIETY *OVERCOMING THE PITFALLS OF PROJECT LAUNCHES*	47
CHAPTER NINE	THE GLOBAL SUPER BUYER *USING AI TO FIND CUSTOMERS ANYWHERE*	53
CHAPTER TEN	THE UNSTOPPABLE MARCH OF AI *THE FUTURE IS HERE... NOW*	59
AFTERWORD		67

DEDICATIONS

THE FUTURE IS NOW

In under 1,000 days, the unstoppable march of AI will transform the world of work and revolutionize the real estate industry. In a world of daunting and rapid change, these inspirational change leaders are showing us the way. We pay tribute to their vision, courage, passion, and their ability to execute as they lead us all into a brave new world powered by AI.

Sam Altman

The visionary entrepreneur and investor is revolutionizing the world of artificial intelligence as the dynamic CEO of OpenAI. Formerly the trailblazing president of Y Combinator, he continues to shape the future of technology with his groundbreaking innovations across all industries.

Elon Musk

The audacious mastermind behind SpaceX and Tesla is pushing the boundaries of space travel and electric vehicles. With his relentless pursuit of innovation, he's transforming our future, one groundbreaking venture at a time. His focus on AI and humanoid robotics is set to change the game for the two worlds of business and real estate, and how we work.

Naval Ravikant

The enigmatic entrepreneur and angel investor is redefining the realms of wealth and wisdom with his profound insights. As the co-founder of AngelList, he's a guiding force for countless startups and a beacon of modern philosophical thought.

Paul Graham

The legendary co-founder of Y Combinator is a titan in the startup world, known for turning visionary ideas into billion-dollar enterprises. His essays and mentorship have inspired a generation of entrepreneurs to chase their wildest dreams.

Mohamed Alabbar

The mastermind behind Emaar Properties UAE is reshaping the world with iconic marvels like the Burj Khalifa and Dubai Mall. His visionary leadership in real estate is revolutionizing urban landscapes and setting new standards of luxury and innovation globally. His deep interest in technology is leading the way and showcasing the future of real estate development.

Finally, a quick word of gratitude and appreciation to all the remarkable individuals whose unwavering support and steadfastness through thick and thin have been inspirational. To the friends, colleagues, investors, and partners who have knowingly or unknowingly contributed to this book, I say thank you!

To Rishi Khosla, Vinod K. Khanna, Riju Jhunjhunwala, Harold Gittelmon, and Paul Marson-Smith—your qualities of decency, faith, friendship, and belief have been invaluable. If the Gen AI that is about to govern the world can be half as special as all of you, the world shall be happier than it has ever been.

Thank you for your friendship and faith!

PREFACE

This book is the culmination of extensive research, countless conversations with industry experts, and a deep dive into the transformative power of artificial intelligence (AI) in the real estate sector. The journey we've embarked upon is nothing short of revolutionary, and I'm thrilled to share it with you.

Real estate, for many of us, is not just about buildings and transactions; it's about dreams, aspirations, and significant life milestones. Whether it's buying your first home, investing in commercial properties, or managing vast real estate portfolios, the stakes are high, and the impact is profound. Yet, despite its importance, the industry has long been plagued by inefficiencies, outdated practices, and a slow adoption of technological advancements. But change is on the horizon, and that change is being driven by AI.

When we talk about AI in real estate, we're not just referring to automated chatbots or basic data analysis. We're delving into a sophisticated ecosystem where machine learning algorithms can predict market trends with astonishing accuracy, where AI-powered robots can guide potential buyers through property tours, and where humanistic AI can understand and respond to customer emotions and preferences. This is the new frontier of real estate, and it's happening right now.

Imagine a world where the vast majority of real estate leads don't fall through the cracks but are nurtured and converted with the precision and efficiency only AI can provide. Traditional methods, reliant on manual processes and broad, untargeted marketing, have left us with a staggering 98% of potential deals never reaching fruition. This colossal waste of time, money, and effort is being transformed by AI technologies that streamline every aspect of the sales process, from lead generation to closing deals. AI can analyze vast amounts of data to identify high-potential leads, automate follow-ups, and even provide personalized sales scripts, turning the old spray-and-pray marketing model on its head.

Trust has always been a cornerstone of real estate transactions, yet historically, it has been one of the industry's most significant challenges. Buyers often approach property purchases with a mix of excitement and anxiety, wary of misinformation and hidden pitfalls. AI is poised to rebuild this trust by providing perfect information at every step. With AI, prospective buyers can access accurate market trends, price predictions, legal ownership details, and tax implications instantly. This transparency is not just a promise; it's already happening. By empowering buyers with reliable information, AI fosters a transparent ecosystem that can transform the real estate market.

The landscape of digital marketing has also been forever changed. In the past, digital marketing efforts were often blunt instruments, casting wide nets in the hope of catching a few interested buyers. This approach enriched technology giants but offered poor returns for real estate developers. AI brings a level of precision to digital marketing that was previously unattainable. It builds prospective audiences, automates and digitizes marketing processes, and constructs detailed electronic personas of ideal customers, allowing for laser-focused targeting.

By accessing vast amounts of social media and contact information, AI can sort and target high-potential customers within seconds, ensuring that marketing efforts are both efficient and effective.

One of the most thrilling advancements is the potential of AI-powered robots in real estate sales. These aren't just futuristic gadgets; they are practical tools that can manage large volumes of customer interactions with an unprecedented level of consistency and accuracy.

Humanoid robots equipped with advanced conversational AI can handle inquiries, provide detailed property information, and even assist in negotiations. Their novelty draws customers and their efficiency keeps them engaged, offering a blend of human touch and machine precision that is redefining the whole sales process—from start to finish.

As we move forward, the ability to market properties globally has become a reality. Real estate is no longer a local game; it's a global marketplace. With AI, developers can identify and reach potential buyers across the world. Tools like AI-powered translation and time zone management ensure seamless communication, making it easier to engage with buyers from different regions. This global approach expands market reach, diversifies risks and stabilizes sales outcomes.

The direct-to-consumer (D2C) model, empowered by AI, is another paradigm shift. By eliminating intermediaries, developers can control the entire sales process, from prospecting to closing deals. AI-driven marketing platforms, CRM systems, and automated follow-up tools make this model highly efficient and effective. The cost savings from reduced commission payments and the ability to maintain direct relationships with buyers are compelling advantages that are driving the adoption of the D2C model.

Moreover, AI's potential to enhance the buyer experience is unparalleled. Virtual reality (VR) and augmented reality (AR) technologies, powered by AI, are providing immersive property tours that allow buyers to explore properties in detail from anywhere in the world. These technologies offer a level of engagement and transparency that traditional methods cannot match. Buyers can visualize themselves in the property, understand its features and layout, and make informed decisions with greater confidence.

The impact of AI on real estate extends beyond sales and marketing. AI-driven data analytics provides developers with deeper insights into market trends, buyer behaviors, and property performance. These insights inform strategic decisions, from project design and development to pricing and marketing strategies. By leveraging AI, developers can stay ahead of market trends, identify new opportunities, and mitigate risks more effectively.

The integration of AI with other advanced technologies like blockchain and the Internet of Things (IoT) is further enhancing its capabilities. Blockchain technology offers greater transparency and security in real estate transactions, while IoT devices provide real-time data on property conditions and performance.

Together, these technologies are creating a more interconnected real estate ecosystem.

As we look ahead, it's clear that the future of real estate is being shaped by the unstoppable march of AI. The technologies we've discussed are not just futuristic concepts—they are here now, actively transforming the industry. For those who believe that these advancements are far off, it's time to recognize that the future is already upon us. The real estate industry is on the brink of a massive transformation, and those who embrace AI will be well-positioned to lead the way into the future.

The advancements in AI will continue to accelerate, bringing about a new era of growth, innovation, and success for those who are ready to embrace the change. The future is here, and it is unstoppable. By working together, humans and robots can create a more efficient, transparent, and customer-centric real estate market. As we embrace this new era, the possibilities for innovation and growth are limitless. The future is now, and those who adapt to this new reality will lead the way in shaping the future of real estate sales.

CHAPTER ONE

WHY AI? FIXING THE 98% PROBLEM

Real estate has always been a numbers game. The industry thrives on the principle of generating as many leads as possible, knowing that only a small fraction will convert into actual sales. For decades, this model has driven real estate agents to adopt a wide array of lead generation strategies, many of which are time-consuming, labor-intensive, and often inefficient.

Among these traditional methods, cold calling, print advertising, and open houses have been the stalwarts, each contributing to the seemingly insurmountable 98% problem. The 98% problem, simply put, is the harsh reality that in traditional real estate practices, only about 2% of leads convert into successful transactions. This means that a staggering 98% of efforts, time, and resources are essentially wasted.

To understand the gravity of this issue, consider the daily routine of a typical real estate agent: hours spent on the phone cold calling potential leads, distributing flyers and brochures, and hosting open houses that attract more window shoppers than serious buyers. The return on investment (ROI) in these methods is dismally low, yet they have remained the cornerstone of lead generation in real estate. However, the advent of artificial intelligence (AI) is poised to revolutionize this landscape, promising not only to reduce the 98% wastage but also to transform how leads are generated, qualified, and nurtured.

Artificial intelligence is transforming industries across the board, and real estate is no exception. The integration of AI into lead generation and qualification processes is addressing the 98% problem head-on, offering innovative solutions that are both efficient and effective.

Traditional methods of lead generation and management, often described as a "spray and pray" approach, scatter resources widely in the hope of hitting a few targets. This chapter explores the roots of this problem and introduces how artificial intelligence (AI) is set to revolutionize the industry by addressing this inefficiency.

Real estate marketing has long been dominated by a scattergun approach. Companies "spray" their marketing messages broadly through various channels—cold calling, print advertising, open houses—hoping that some of these efforts will "pray" into successful leads.

This approach is akin to throwing darts in the dark, hoping one might hit the bullseye. The inefficiency is glaring: countless hours spent on phone calls that lead nowhere, thousands of dollars invested in ads that go unnoticed, and numerous open houses that attract more curious onlookers than serious buyers. The core issue with the spray and pray model is its lack of precision. Marketing efforts are not targeted, resulting in a low return on investment (ROI). For every hundred potential leads generated, only two may convert into actual deals, leaving the vast majority as wasted opportunities.

Artificial intelligence offers a promising solution to the 98% problem by transforming how real estate transactions are managed across all stages. AI technologies and predictive analytics can dramatically improve the conversion rate from initial interest to closed deals. AI has the potential to manage and optimize all six stages of a real estate transaction: lead generation, lead qualification, client management, property matching, negotiation, and closing.

Each of these stages traditionally involves significant manual effort, time, and resources, often leading to inefficiencies and missed opportunities. By automating and enhancing these stages, AI can significantly reduce the inefficiencies inherent in traditional methods, transforming the entire real estate process into a more streamlined, effective, and profitable operation.

Lead generation is the first and one of the most critical stages in the real estate transaction process. Traditionally, this involved methods such as cold calling, distributing flyers, placing ads in newspapers, and hosting open houses. These methods are time-consuming, labor-intensive, and often yield low conversion rates. AI, however, can transform lead generation by using machine learning algorithms to analyze vast amounts of data, including online behavior, social media activity, and historical transaction records. This analysis can identify potential clients who are more likely to be interested in buying or selling a property, enabling agents to target their efforts more precisely and effectively.

Once leads are generated, the next challenge is to qualify them. Traditional methods rely on manual assessment and intuition, which can be time-consuming and inaccurate. AI can streamline this process through predictive analytics, scoring leads based on their likelihood to convert. By analyzing factors such as past behavior, engagement level, and market conditions, AI can prioritize high-quality leads, ensuring that agents focus their efforts on the most promising prospects, thereby improving conversion rates and reducing wasted effort.

Effective client management is crucial for maintaining relationships and closing deals. Traditional Customer Relationship Management (CRM) systems often fall short because they provide retrospective data rather than real-time insights. In an era where the pace of business has accelerated dramatically, these clunky systems are no longer sufficient. AI-driven CRM systems, on the other hand, offer real-time analysis and predictive analytics, allowing agents to manage their client interactions more proactively.

These systems can analyze client behavior and preferences, offer personalized engagement strategies, and automate routine tasks, thereby freeing up agents to focus on high-value activities such as building relationships and closing deals.

Matching clients with the right properties is a critical step in the real estate process. Traditionally, this involved agents manually sifting through property listings to find matches based on client preferences. AI can enhance this process by analyzing a client's preferences and behavior to recommend properties that are a perfect fit. Advanced algorithms can consider a wide range of factors, including location, price, amenities, and client-specific needs, to provide more accurate and personalized recommendations. Additionally, virtual tours and augmented reality (AR) applications powered by AI can offer clients immersive property views remotely, further enhancing the matching process.

Negotiation is an art that requires skill and data-driven insights. AI can assist in the negotiation process by analyzing market trends, property values, and buyer behavior to provide data-driven recommendations.

AI tools can suggest optimal pricing strategies, identify potential negotiation points, and predict the outcomes of different negotiation tactics. This helps agents negotiate more effectively, ensuring better deals for their clients and increasing the likelihood of successful transactions.

The closing stage of a real estate transaction involves numerous administrative tasks, from document management to contract generation. Traditionally, these tasks are manual and time-consuming, often leading to delays and errors. AI can automate many of these tasks, streamlining the closing process and reducing the time and effort required to complete a transaction. AI-powered tools can generate contracts, manage documents, schedule inspections, and ensure all necessary steps are completed accurately and on time. This not only speeds up the closing process but also improves the overall client experience by providing a more seamless and efficient transaction.

Traditional CRM systems, while valuable in their time, have become akin to trying to drive by looking in the rearview mirror. They provide historical data on client interactions but fail to offer actionable insights for future actions. In an era where the pace of business has accelerated dramatically, these systems are no longer sufficient. The shift from traditional CRM systems to AI-driven CRM represents a significant evolution in client management. AI-driven CRM systems offer real-time data analysis, predictive analytics, and automated workflows, transforming how agents interact with clients.

AI systems can analyze vast amounts of client data to identify patterns and trends, providing agents with actionable insights. They can match leads with the most suitable salesperson based on their expertise and past performance, identify buying patterns and predict future actions, recommend personalized sales approaches and scripts, manage follow-ups, oversee the entire sales process from initial contact to closing, help with negotiations by analyzing market data and client behavior, and monitor the entire sales cycle in real-time.

Unlike traditional CRM systems, AI-driven CRM looks forward, not backward. It helps agents anticipate client needs, respond proactively and make data-driven decisions. This shift from a retrospective to a prospective approach is crucial in reducing the 98% wastage and improving overall efficiency. To illustrate the transformative potential of AI in real estate, let's examine a case study of how a technology-driven real estate brokerage, Compass, has integrated AI into its operations. Compass uses an AI-powered platform to enhance its lead generation and client management processes.

The platform analyzes vast amounts of data to identify high-potential leads and provide agents with actionable insights. By targeting high-quality leads and offering personalized recommendations, Compass has significantly improved its conversion rates. Moreover, the use of AI-driven CRM systems and virtual assistants has streamlined operations, allowing agents to focus on building relationships and closing deals. This has not only increased productivity but also enhanced the overall client experience.

The success of Compass demonstrates the potential of AI to address the 98% problem in real estate. By leveraging AI to generate and qualify leads more efficiently, real estate professionals can reduce wastage and improve their overall productivity and profitability. The integration of AI into real estate is still in its early stages, but the potential for growth and innovation is immense. As AI technology continues to evolve, its applications in real estate will expand, offering new opportunities for efficiency and effectiveness.

One promising area of development is the use of AI to analyze and predict property values. By leveraging machine learning algorithms and big data, AI can provide more accurate and timely property valuations, helping buyers and sellers make informed decisions. This could revolutionize the appraisal process, reducing the reliance on manual assessments and improving the accuracy of property valuations. AI-powered tools can automate many of the administrative tasks involved in buying and selling a property, from document management to contract generation. This could significantly reduce the time and effort required to complete a transaction, improving the efficiency of the real estate process.

The integration of AI with other emerging technologies, such as blockchain and the Internet of Things (IoT), could further enhance the real estate industry. Blockchain technology can provide a secure and transparent way to manage property transactions, while IoT devices can provide real-time data on property conditions and usage. By combining these technologies with AI, real estate professionals can offer more comprehensive and innovative solutions to their clients.

The 98% problem has long plagued the real estate industry, resulting in a colossal waste of marketing dollars and man-hours. Traditional lead generation methods, characterized by the spray and pray approach, are inefficient and yield low conversion rates. However, the advent of artificial intelligence offers a promising solution to this problem.

AI has the potential to revolutionize all stages of a real estate transaction, from lead generation to closing. By leveraging AI-powered tools and predictive analytics, real estate professionals can significantly improve their conversion rates and reduce wastage. AI-driven CRM systems provide real-time insights and proactive recommendations, enhancing client management and overall efficiency.

As AI technology continues to evolve, its applications in real estate will expand, offering new opportunities for innovation and growth. By embracing AI, real estate professionals can address the 98% problem head-on, transforming how leads are generated, qualified, and nurtured, and ultimately improving the productivity and profitability of the industry.

The future of real estate lies in the integration of advanced technologies, and those who adopt AI early will be at the forefront of this transformative wave, setting new standards for efficiency and success in the industry.

CHAPTER TWO

BUILDING BRIDGES OF TRUST
THE POWER OF AI AND PERFECT INFORMATION

The real estate industry has long been plagued by a pervasive trust deficit. Despite its crucial role in shaping lives and communities, real estate remains one of the least trusted sectors. This mistrust stems from a combination of historical practices, lack of transparency, and the complex, high-stakes nature of real estate transactions. In a recent survey, real estate agents were ranked among the least trustworthy professionals, alongside used car salesmen.

This deep-seated skepticism leads customers to delay and defer purchase decisions as they double-check and verify the information provided to them. This prolonged decision-making cycle not only frustrates potential buyers but also hampers the efficiency and profitability of the real estate market.

In this context, the advent of AI offers a revolutionary solution. AI can provide perfect decision-making information to potential property buyers, fundamentally altering how trust is built and maintained in the real estate ecosystem. By leveraging AI technologies, market trends, price predictions, legal ownership queries, title insurance issues, tax questions, and maintenance concerns can all be addressed with unprecedented accuracy and reliability. This comprehensive and accurate information is crucial in fostering trust and speeding up the decision-making process.

Artificial intelligence's ability to provide perfect information stems from its capacity to analyze vast amounts of data from multiple domains simultaneously. AI systems, particularly those based on advanced models like PropGPT and large language models (LLMs), can synthesize data from diverse sources to offer precise, real-time insights.

For instance, market trends can be predicted with high accuracy by analyzing historical sales data, current market conditions, and economic indicators. Price predictions can be fine-tuned by considering factors such as neighborhood developments, local amenities, and future growth prospects. These predictive capabilities of AI can significantly enhance the confidence of potential buyers in the information provided to them.

One of the critical areas where AI can build trust is in answering legal ownership and title insurance questions. Real estate transactions are fraught with legal complexities, and any uncertainty in ownership or title can be a major deterrent for buyers.

AI can streamline this process by accessing and analyzing public records, historical transaction data, and legal documents to verify ownership and ensure that there are no encumbrances on the property. This capability not only provides peace of mind to buyers but also reduces the risk of legal disputes post-purchase.

Tax-related queries are another significant concern for property buyers. Understanding the tax implications of a real estate transaction, including property taxes, capital gains tax, and potential tax benefits, requires a nuanced understanding of tax laws and regulations. AI can demystify this aspect by providing accurate, personalized tax information based on the buyer's financial situation and the specific property in question. This level of precision helps buyers make informed decisions, thereby fostering trust in the transaction process.

Maintenance is another area where AI can play a pivotal role in building trust. Potential buyers often worry about the long-term upkeep and maintenance costs associated with a property. AI can address these concerns by analyzing the property's condition, historical maintenance records, and expected future repairs. By providing a detailed maintenance forecast, AI helps buyers understand the true cost of ownership, enabling them to make more confident and informed decisions.

The role of AI in building trust in the real estate system cannot be overstated. By offering perfect knowledge across various domains, AI alleviates the uncertainties and risks that typically accompany real estate transactions. This newfound transparency and reliability speed up the decision-making cycle, as buyers no longer need to spend excessive time verifying information.

Those developers and real estate professionals who embrace AI's ability to provide perfect knowledge stand to gain rich rewards in the form of increased sales and enhanced customer satisfaction.

PropGPT and LLMs are at the forefront of this transformation. These advanced AI models are designed to handle the vast and varied data associated with real estate transactions. They can interpret and analyze complex datasets, generate accurate predictions, and provide detailed, context-specific insights. For example, PropGPT can offer a comprehensive overview of a property, including its market value, ownership history, legal status, and future price trends. This level of detail helps buyers feel more secure in their decisions, knowing that they are based on reliable, data-driven insights.

The impact of AI on the sales cycle of real estate is profound. By serving as a reliable source of correct information, AI reduces the time buyers spend on due diligence. When buyers trust the information provided to them, they are more likely to make quicker decisions. This acceleration in the decision-making process not only benefits buyers but also enhances the efficiency of the entire real estate market. Faster sales cycles mean that properties spend less time on the market, reducing holding costs for sellers and increasing the overall turnover rate.

Moreover, the trust generated by AI extends beyond individual transactions. As buyers experience the benefits of AI-powered insights, their overall trust in the real estate system grows. This cumulative effect can lead to a more transparent and efficient market, where information asymmetry is minimized, and trust is the norm rather than the exception.

Developers who harness the power of AI to provide perfect information to property customers will be at a significant advantage. They will be able to offer a superior customer experience, characterized by transparency, accuracy, and reliability. This not only attracts more buyers but also fosters long-term relationships based on trust. In a market where reputation is critical, the ability to consistently provide perfect information can set a developer apart from the competition and lead to sustained success. The integration of AI in real estate also has broader implications for the industry. It can help standardize information practices, leading to a more cohesive and reliable market. As AI systems become more widespread, they can establish industry benchmarks for data accuracy and transparency. This, in turn, can drive regulatory changes that further enhance trust and efficiency in the real estate market.

However, the adoption of AI is not without challenges. Real estate professionals need to be adequately trained to use AI tools effectively. There is also a need for robust data governance frameworks to ensure that the data used by AI systems is accurate, secure, and compliant with privacy regulations. Despite these challenges, the potential benefits of AI far outweigh the hurdles. By embracing AI, the real estate industry can overcome its trust deficit and build a more transparent, efficient, and trustworthy market.

As AI continues to evolve, its impact on the real estate industry will only grow, paving the way for a more transparent, efficient, and trustworthy market.

CHAPTER THREE

THE DEATH OF DIGITAL MARKETING
LASER-FOCUSED AI PROSPECTING IS THE FUTURE

In today's fast-paced, technology-driven world, digital marketing on social media and search engines, coupled with portal listings, has become the cornerstone of lead generation in the real estate industry. However, this method, while seemingly advanced, is an extremely blunt weapon. It targets millions in the hopes of finding one potential buyer, resulting in inefficiencies and exorbitant costs that ultimately benefit technology giants more than the real estate professionals themselves.

The traditional digital marketing approach, though widely adopted, provides poor results due to its inherent lack of precision. Despite its suboptimal nature, the absence of a viable alternative has led real estate professionals to flock to these methods, perpetuating a cycle of inefficiency and waste.

The fundamental issue with digital marketing in real estate lies in its broad, indiscriminate approach. Digital ads on social media platforms and search engines are designed to reach vast audiences, casting a wide net in the hope of catching a few interested parties. This method, while increasing visibility, does not guarantee that the right audience is being targeted.

The result is a significant amount of marketing spend that reaches individuals who have no intention or interest in purchasing property. This shotgun approach leads to a low conversion rate, with a significant portion of the marketing budget essentially going to waste. Moreover, the reliance on technology giants for digital marketing further exacerbates the problem. Companies like Google and Facebook dominate the digital advertising space, commanding high prices for their services. While these platforms offer unparalleled reach and sophisticated targeting options, they also prioritize their own profitability. The algorithms and pricing structures are designed to maximize revenue for these companies, often at the expense of advertisers. This dynamic results in an ongoing cycle where real estate professionals spend vast sums on digital marketing campaigns that yield minimal returns, enriching the technology giants in the process.

In contrast to the broad and inefficient traditional digital marketing methods, AI offers a revolutionary alternative. AI can build prospective audiences, automate and digitize marketing processes, create electronic personas of ideal customers, and then source and target these individuals online with incredible precision, all within seconds. This laser-focused approach stands in stark contrast to the blunt weapon of traditional digital marketing, promising to transform how real estate professionals engage with potential buyers.

AI-driven marketing begins with the creation of detailed electronic personas of ideal customers. By analyzing vast amounts of data, AI can identify the characteristics, behaviors, and preferences of individuals who are most likely to be interested in a particular property. This process involves aggregating data from various sources, including social media profiles, online behavior, past purchasing history, and even demographic information. The result is a highly detailed and accurate profile of potential buyers, allowing for more targeted and effective marketing efforts.

Once these personas are established, AI can source and target these individuals online with unparalleled precision. By accessing social media and contact information, AI can identify and engage with potential buyers who match the ideal customer profile. This process involves sophisticated algorithms that can filter through vast amounts of data to identify high-potential customers. The targeting is not just broad but finely tuned to reach individuals who are most likely to be interested in the properties being marketed.

The automation capabilities of AI further enhance its effectiveness in real estate marketing. AI can manage the exchange of information with potential buyers, ensuring that they receive relevant and timely communication. From initial contact to follow-up, AI can handle the entire communication process, providing personalized and responsive interactions that build trust and engagement. This automated approach not only saves time but also ensures that no potential lead falls through the cracks.

Moreover, AI can ensure sufficient follow-up with potential buyers. One of the critical aspects of successful real estate marketing is maintaining engagement with interested parties. Traditional methods often fall short in this regard, as manual follow-up can be inconsistent and prone to human error. AI, on the other hand, can track interactions and schedule follow-ups automatically, ensuring that potential buyers remain engaged and informed throughout the process. This continuous engagement increases the likelihood of conversion, as buyers are more likely to proceed with a purchase when they feel valued and well-informed.

The impact of AI on real estate marketing extends beyond individual transactions. By leveraging AI, real estate professionals can gain deeper insights into market trends and buyer behavior. This information can inform broader marketing strategies, helping to optimize campaigns and improve overall effectiveness. AI can analyze data on a macro level, identifying patterns and trends that may not be immediately apparent through traditional methods. These insights can guide marketing efforts, ensuring that resources are allocated more effectively and that campaigns are tailored to meet the market's needs.

The transformative potential of AI in real estate marketing cannot be overstated. Traditional digital marketing methods, with their broad and indiscriminate approach, are increasingly being recognized as outdated and inefficient. AI offers a precise, targeted alternative that can significantly enhance the effectiveness of marketing efforts. By building detailed customer personas, targeting high-potential buyers, automating communication, and ensuring consistent follow-up, AI can dramatically improve conversion rates and reduce wasted spend.

Furthermore, the cost-efficiency of AI-driven marketing is a significant advantage. Traditional digital marketing campaigns often require substantial investment, with a significant portion of the budget going to technology giants like Google and Facebook. AI-driven marketing, on the other hand, can achieve better results with a fraction of the cost. By targeting the right audience and automating processes, AI reduces the need for extensive manual intervention and minimizes wasted spend. This cost-efficiency is particularly valuable in a competitive market, where maximizing ROI is crucial for success.

The future of real estate marketing lies in the adoption of AI and other advanced technologies. As AI continues to evolve, its capabilities will only improve, offering even greater precision and effectiveness. Real estate professionals who embrace these technologies will be at the forefront of the industry, setting new standards for marketing excellence. By moving away from blunt digital marketing methods and adopting laser-focused AI prospecting, real estate industry can overcome the inefficiencies of the past and build a more efficient and profitable future.

AI-driven marketing platforms are capable of integrating with multiple data sources, providing a holistic view of potential buyers. This integration allows AI to continuously update and refine customer personas based on real-time data. For instance, if a potential buyer exhibits new online behaviors or preferences, AI can adjust its targeting strategies accordingly. This dynamic approach ensures that marketing efforts remain relevant and effective, adapting to the changing needs and preferences of potential buyers.

In addition to improving targeting and personalization, AI can also enhance the creative aspects of marketing. AI-powered tools can generate content, design ads, and even optimize the timing and placement of marketing messages. By analyzing the performance of different creative elements, AI can identify which approaches resonate most with potential buyers, enabling marketers to refine their strategies and maximize engagement. This level of optimization is difficult to achieve through traditional methods, highlighting another key advantage of AI-driven marketing.

The benefits of AI in real estate marketing extend to customer service as well. AI-powered chatbots and virtual assistants can provide instant, personalized responses to inquiries, guiding potential buyers through the initial stages of their property search. These tools can answer questions, provide property recommendations, and schedule viewings, all while offering a seamless and user-friendly experience. By handling routine inquiries and tasks, AI frees up real estate professionals to focus on more complex and high-value activities, such as negotiations and relationship building.

As AI continues to transform real estate marketing, it is also fostering greater transparency and trust within the industry. Traditional digital marketing methods often leave buyers feeling skeptical about the accuracy and reliability of the information they receive. In contrast, AI-driven marketing provides data-backed insights that are more likely to inspire confidence. By delivering precise and relevant information, AI helps build trust between buyers and sellers, facilitating smoother and more successful transactions.

The shift towards AI-driven marketing is also influencing the competitive landscape of the real estate industry. Early adopters of AI technology are gaining a significant edge, attracting more buyers and closing deals faster than their competitors. This competitive advantage is driving broader adoption of AI, as more real estate professionals recognize the need to innovate and stay ahead in a rapidly evolving market. Over time, AI is expected to become a standard tool in real estate marketing, raising the level of effectiveness across the industry.

Despite the clear advantages of AI, its adoption in real estate marketing is not without challenges. Real estate professionals need to be adequately trained to use AI tools effectively, and there is a need for robust data governance frameworks to ensure that the data used by AI systems is accurate, secure, and compliant with privacy regulations. Additionally, integrating AI with existing systems and processes can require significant investment and organizational change. However, the long-term benefits of AI far outweigh these initial hurdles, making it a worthwhile investment for the future.

The traditional approach to digital marketing in real estate, characterized by its broad and indiscriminate targeting, is increasingly being recognized as a blunt and inefficient weapon. This method, while widely adopted, results in significant wasted spend and enriches technology giants at the expense of real estate professionals. AI offers a transformative alternative, providing the precision and efficiency needed to revolutionize real estate marketing.

By building detailed customer personas, targeting high-potential buyers, automating communication, and ensuring consistent follow-up, AI can dramatically improve conversion rates and reduce wasted spend. The future of real estate marketing lies in the adoption of AI and other advanced technologies, paving the way for a more efficient, effective, and profitable industry.

CHAPTER FOUR

DRIVING OFF-PLAN SALES
LEARNING TO FLY WITH AI

At the center of the real estate ecosystem lies the real estate developer, a pivotal player whose success or failure can have a cascading impact on the entire market. Real estate developers face numerous challenges, but among the most daunting is the complexity of marketing new launch projects.

The need to sell large amounts of inventory, often worth millions or even billions, within a very short period of time presents a unique set of hurdles. To overcome this enormous task, developers must rely on an infrastructure that operates like a well-oiled machine, enabling them to sell hundreds of homes within weeks or months. However, the processes involved in these launches are complex and challenging, often leading to significant stress and inefficiencies when managed solely by humans.

The traditional approach to marketing new real estate projects involves a flood of marketing activities, intensive sales follow-up processes, and a meticulous orchestration of various tasks to ensure a successful launch. This manual, human-driven effort is prone to errors, inconsistencies, and inefficiencies. The pressure to perform flawlessly under tight deadlines can cause significant strain, often resulting in suboptimal outcomes.

This is where AI comes into play, offering a solution that can take over from the overdependence on humans for executing large-scale project launches.

AI can fine-tune the approach to marketing and managing new real estate projects, ensuring clean digital efficiency throughout the entire process. By leveraging AI, developers can streamline operations, enhance precision, and ultimately drive better outcomes in their off-plan sales efforts. Let's explore how AI is revolutionizing the way real estate developers market and sell new projects, transforming the industry and enabling developers to "learn to fly" with AI.

The launch of a new real estate project is a monumental undertaking that requires meticulous planning, coordination, and execution. Traditionally, this process has been managed by teams of marketing professionals, sales agents, and project managers, each responsible for different aspects of the launch. The marketing team must develop and execute a comprehensive strategy to generate interest and attract potential buyers.

This involves creating advertising campaigns, organizing events, and leveraging various marketing channels to reach the target audience. The sales team, on the other hand, must handle inquiries, conduct follow-ups, and close deals, often working under immense pressure to meet sales targets. Meanwhile, project managers oversee the entire process, ensuring that all tasks are completed on time and within budget.

This human-driven approach, while effective to some extent, is fraught with challenges. The sheer volume of tasks, coupled with the need for precision and speed, can lead to errors and inefficiencies. Miscommunication between teams, missed follow-ups, and inconsistent customer experiences are common issues that can derail a project launch. Moreover, the reliance on manual processes makes it difficult to adapt to changing market conditions or buyer preferences.

AI addresses these challenges by automating and optimizing various aspects of the project launch process. One of the key areas where AI can make a significant impact is in marketing. AI-powered marketing platforms can analyze vast amounts of data to identify the most effective strategies for reaching the target audience. By examining factors such as buyer behavior, market trends, and demographic information, AI can develop highly targeted marketing campaigns that are more likely to resonate with potential buyers. These campaigns can be executed across multiple channels, including social media, search engines, and email, ensuring maximum reach and engagement.

In addition to creating targeted marketing campaigns, AI can also optimize the timing and placement of advertisements. By analyzing data on buyer activity and engagement patterns, AI can determine the optimal times to run ads and the best platforms to use. This level of precision ensures that marketing efforts are not wasted on audiences that are unlikely to convert, thereby improving the overall efficiency of the campaign.

AI also plays a crucial role in managing the sales process. One of the most significant challenges in off-plan sales is handling the volume of inquiries and follow-ups. Potential buyers often require detailed information about the project, including floor plans, pricing, and amenities. Manually responding to these inquiries can be time-consuming and prone to delays. AI-powered chatbots and virtual assistants can handle these tasks efficiently, providing instant responses to common questions and guiding buyers through the initial stages of the sales process. These tools can also schedule follow-up appointments and reminders, ensuring that no lead is left unattended.

Moreover, AI can analyze buyer interactions and behaviors to identify high-potential leads. By examining factors such as the frequency and nature of inquiries, AI can determine which buyers are most likely to convert and prioritize them for follow-up. This targeted approach ensures that sales agents focus their efforts on the most promising leads, improving the likelihood of closing deals.

Another area where AI can drive efficiency is in the management of customer relationships. Traditional customer relationship management (CRM) systems, while useful, are often limited by their reliance on manual data entry and retrospective analysis. AI-driven CRM systems, on the other hand, offer real-time data analysis and incredible predictive insights.

By continuously analyzing customer interactions and engagement patterns, AI can provide actionable recommendations for personalized communication and follow-up strategies. This proactive approach helps build stronger relationships with potential buyers, enhancing their overall experience and increasing the likelihood of conversion.

AI's ability to handle large volumes of data and automate complex processes extends beyond marketing and sales. Project management, a critical aspect of any estate launch, can also benefit from AI-driven solutions. AI-powered project management tools can streamline the coordination of tasks, monitor progress in real-time, and identify potential bottlenecks. By providing a centralized platform for managing all aspects of the project, these tools ensure that teams remain aligned and that deadlines are met. This level of oversight and control reduces the risk of errors and delays, ensuring a smooth and efficient project launch.

Furthermore, AI can enhance decision-making by providing developers with valuable insights into market trends and buyer preferences. By analyzing data from past projects, current market conditions, and competitor activities, AI can identify emerging trends and opportunities.

This information allows developers to make informed decisions about pricing, marketing strategies, and project features, ensuring that their offerings align with market demands. The ability to adapt quickly to changing conditions gives developers a competitive edge, increasing their chances of success in the highly competitive real estate market.

The integration of AI into the project launch process also brings significant benefits in terms of scalability. Traditional methods of managing project launches are often limited by the availability of human resources and the capacity to handle large volumes of tasks. AI, however, can scale effortlessly to accommodate projects of any size. Whether it's managing inquiries for a small development or coordinating the launch of a large-scale project, AI can handle the workload efficiently, ensuring that all tasks are completed on time and to a high standard.

One of the most exciting aspects of AI in real estate is its potential to enhance the buyer experience. Off-plan sales often involve a degree of uncertainty for buyers, as they are purchasing a property that has not yet been built.

AI can mitigate this uncertainty by providing buyers with detailed, accurate, and up-to-date information about the project. Virtual reality (VR) and augmented reality (AR) technologies, powered by AI, can offer immersive virtual tours of the property, allowing buyers to visualize their future home. These technologies can also provide real-time updates on the progress of the construction, keeping buyers informed and engaged throughout the process.

Additionally, AI can personalize the buying experience by tailoring communication and recommendations to the individual preferences of each buyer. By analyzing data on buyer behavior and preferences, AI can suggest properties, features, and financing options that are most likely to appeal to each buyer. This level of personalization enhances the buyer experience, making them feel valued and understood, and increasing their confidence in the purchase decision.

The benefits of AI in driving off-plan sales extend to all stakeholders in the real estate ecosystem. For developers, AI offers a more efficient and effective way to manage project launches, reducing the reliance on manual processes and minimizing the risk of errors. For sales agents, AI provides valuable support in handling inquiries, prioritizing leads, and managing follow-ups, enabling them to focus on building relationships and closing deals. For buyers, AI offers a more transparent, personalized, and engaging experience, reducing uncertainty and increasing confidence in their purchase decision.

As AI continues to evolve, its impact on the real estate industry will only grow. Developers who embrace AI and integrate it into their project launch processes will be well-positioned to succeed in the competitive real estate market. By leveraging AI to streamline operations, enhance precision, and improve the buyer experience, developers can achieve better outcomes and drive greater success in their off-plan sales efforts.

The future of real estate lies in the integration of advanced technologies, and AI is at the forefront of this transformation. By learning to fly with AI, developers can navigate the complexities of off-plan sales with greater ease and efficiency, unlocking new opportunities for success.

The challenges faced by real estate developers in marketing and selling new launch projects are significant, but AI offers a powerful solution. By automating and optimizing various aspects of the project launch process, AI can drive efficiency, enhance precision, and improve outcomes.

CHAPTER FIVE

THE INCREDIBLE AI MIND READER
THE POWER OF HUMANISTIC TECHNOLOGY

As mentioned in previous chapters, an overwhelming 98% of real estate transactions fail to close. This staggering statistic translates to vast amounts of wasted time, effort, and resources. The real estate industry, traditionally reliant on manual processes and broad marketing strategies, has long struggled with inefficiencies that hinder optimal performance. However, a new and incredible branch of artificial intelligence, known as humanistic AI, has made significant strides in addressing these challenges.

This innovative technology has the potential to revolutionize the way property professionals interact with potential customers by reading emotional states and predicting behavior with remarkable accuracy.

Humanistic AI leverages advanced machine learning algorithms and natural language processing to understand and interpret human emotions and behaviors. This branch of AI goes beyond traditional data analysis by incorporating elements of psychology and behavioral science, enabling it to read and respond to human emotional cues. For real estate professionals, this means gaining unprecedented insights into the minds of potential buyers, allowing for more targeted and effective marketing strategies.

One of the key capabilities of humanistic AI is its ability to gauge interest levels and prioritize high-potential leads.

By analyzing various data points, such as voice samples and written text, humanistic AI can assess a person's emotional state and predict their likelihood of conversion. This allows property professionals to focus their energies on leads with the highest potential for success, thereby increasing efficiency and improving conversion rates.

For example, humanistic AI can analyze a simple voice sample to detect subtle emotional cues that may indicate a person's level of interest or hesitation. Tone of voice, speech patterns, and even pauses can provide valuable information about a person's emotional state.

Similarly, AI can analyze a 500-word text sample authored by a potential buyer to gain insights into their personality, preferences, and motivations. This level of analysis allows real estate professionals to tailor their approach to each individual, creating a more personalized and engaging experience.

As these technologies advance, the filtration process to identify high-prospect leads will continue to improve. Humanistic AI will become increasingly adept at recognizing and interpreting complex emotional signals, further enhancing its predictive capabilities. This will enable property professionals to not only identify high-potential leads but also to understand the underlying motivations and concerns of these individuals. By addressing these factors, real estate agents can build stronger relationships with potential buyers, ultimately leading to higher conversion rates.

The implications of humanistic AI for the real estate industry are profound. By harnessing the power of this technology, property professionals can transform their approach to lead generation and management. Instead of relying on broad and inefficient marketing strategies, they can adopt a more targeted and personalized approach, focusing on the needs and preferences of individual buyers. This shift has the potential to significantly reduce the amount of wasted time and resources, improving overall efficiency and profitability.

The integration of humanistic AI into the real estate process can enhance the customer experience. Potential buyers often feel overwhelmed by the complexity and uncertainty of real estate transactions. Humanistic AI can alleviate these concerns by providing a more personalized and empathetic approach.

By understanding and addressing the emotional states of buyers, property professionals can create a more supportive and reassuring environment, ultimately increasing buyer confidence and satisfaction.

The power of humanistic AI extends beyond lead generation and customer engagement. This technology can also play a crucial role in other aspects of the real estate process, such as negotiation and closing. By analyzing the emotional states of all parties involved, humanistic AI can provide valuable insights that help to facilitate smoother and more effective negotiations. For example, understanding the concerns and motivations of a seller can enable a buyer to tailor their offer in a way that addresses these factors, increasing the likelihood of a successful transaction.

Additionally, humanistic AI can help to identify potential red flags and mitigate risks. By analyzing behavioral patterns and emotional cues, AI can detect signs of hesitation or uncertainty that may indicate potential issues. This allows property professionals to address these concerns proactively, reducing the risk of deals falling through at the last minute.

The integration of humanistic AI into the real estate industry also has the potential to drive significant cultural and operational changes. Traditional real estate practices often prioritize volume over quality, focusing on generating as many leads as possible in the hope that a small percentage will convert. Humanistic AI challenges this approach by emphasizing the importance of understanding and addressing the needs of individual buyers. This shift requires a more empathetic and customer-centric mindset, which can ultimately lead to more meaningful and successful interactions.

Furthermore, the adoption of humanistic AI can lead to more collaborative and transparent relationships between buyers, sellers, and agents. By providing a deeper understanding of the emotional states and motivations of all parties involved, AI can help to build trust and foster open communication. This can create a more positive and supportive environment, ultimately leading to better outcomes for everyone involved.

As humanistic AI continues to evolve, its applications in the real estate industry will expand. Future advancements may include even more sophisticated emotional analysis capabilities, such as the ability to detect micro-expressions and body language cues. These developments will further enhance the predictive power of AI, allowing property professionals to gain even deeper insights into the minds of potential buyers.

In addition to improving lead generation and customer engagement, humanistic AI can also play a crucial role in market analysis and strategy development. By analyzing large volumes of data on buyer behavior and preferences, AI can identify emerging trends and shifts in the market.

This information can inform marketing strategies and help property professionals to stay ahead of the competition. For example, AI can identify patterns in buyer preferences for certain types of properties or locations, enabling developers to tailor their projects to meet these demands.

Moreover, humanistic AI can enhance the accuracy and effectiveness of marketing campaigns. By understanding the emotional triggers that drive buyer behavior, AI can create more compelling and persuasive marketing messages. This can increase engagement and conversion rates, ultimately driving greater success for real estate professionals.

The potential of humanistic AI extends beyond the residential real estate market. Commercial real estate transactions, which often involve complex negotiations and significant financial stakes, can also benefit from the insights provided by AI. Understanding the motivations and concerns of corporate clients can help property professionals to tailor their approach and secure more successful deals. Additionally, AI can assist in managing the relationships between multiple stakeholders, such as investors, tenants, and property managers, ensuring that all parties are aligned and satisfied.

The integration of humanistic AI into the real estate industry also has important implications for training and development. Real estate professionals can benefit from AI-driven training programs that teach them how to interpret and respond to emotional cues. These programs can enhance their communication and negotiation skills, enabling them to build stronger relationships with clients and achieve better outcomes. By combining the analytical power of AI with the interpersonal skills of human agents, the real estate industry can create a more effective and harmonious approach to customer engagement.

Despite the numerous benefits of humanistic AI, its adoption also raises important ethical and privacy considerations. The ability to analyze and interpret emotional states and behavior involves the collection and processing of sensitive personal data. It is essential for real estate professionals to handle this data responsibly, ensuring that privacy and consent are respected. Transparent communication with clients about the use of AI and the data being collected is crucial to building trust and maintaining ethical standards.

Furthermore, the potential for bias in AI algorithms must be addressed. AI systems are trained on large datasets, and if these datasets contain biases, the resulting algorithms may perpetuate or even amplify these biases. This can lead to unfair treatment of certain individuals or groups. It is important for developers and users of humanistic AI to be aware of these risks and to implement measures to mitigate them, such as regular updates of AI models to ensure fairness and accuracy.

Humanistic AI represents a powerful and transformative technology that has the potential to revolutionize the real estate industry. By leveraging advanced machine learning algorithms and natural language processing, humanistic AI can read and respond to human emotions and behaviors with remarkable accuracy.

This enables property professionals to gain unprecedented insights into the minds of potential buyers, allowing for more targeted and effective marketing strategies. The ability to gauge interest levels, prioritize high-potential leads, and provide personalized and empathetic customer engagement can significantly reduce wasted time and resources, improving overall efficiency and profitability.

The integration of humanistic AI into the real estate process can enhance the customer experience, facilitate smoother negotiations, and mitigate risks. It can also drive significant cultural and operational changes, fostering a more customer-centric approach. As AI continues to evolve, its applications in real estate will expand, offering even greater insights and capabilities.

However, the adoption of humanistic AI also raises important ethical and privacy considerations that must be addressed to ensure responsible and fair use of this technology. By handling data responsibly, addressing potential biases, and maintaining transparent communication with clients, the real estate industry can harness the power of humanistic AI to drive innovation and achieve success.

As we look to the future, the potential of humanistic AI to transform the real estate industry is immense. By learning to understand and respond to the emotional states and behaviors of potential buyers, property professionals can build stronger relationships, create more engaging experiences, and achieve higher conversion rates. The power of humanistic technology lies in its ability to bridge the gap between data-driven insights and human empathy, creating a more harmonious and effective approach to real estate transactions. The incredible AI mind reader is not just a tool for improving efficiency; it is a catalyst for building trust, enhancing customer satisfaction, and driving the success of the real estate industry in the years to come.

The transformation enabled by humanistic AI is already beginning to show results. Early adopters of this technology are seeing improvements in lead conversion rates, customer satisfaction, and overall efficiency. As more real estate professionals recognize the benefits of humanistic AI, its adoption will likely accelerate, driving further innovation and improvement within the industry. This shift will not only enhance the performance of individual real estate professionals but also contribute to the overall health and efficiency of the real estate market.

In practical terms, implementing humanistic AI involves several steps. First, real estate companies need to invest in the right AI technologies and platforms. This includes selecting AI tools that can analyze voice samples, text, and other data to interpret emotional states and predict behaviors. Companies also need to ensure that their AI systems are integrated with their existing customer relationship management (CRM) systems and other relevant tools. This integration is crucial for providing a seamless experience and maximizing the benefits of AI.

Next, real estate professionals need to be trained to use humanistic AI effectively. This involves understanding how to interpret AI-generated insights and incorporate them into their day-to-day interactions with clients. Training programs should focus on enhancing communication and negotiation skills, with an emphasis on empathy and understanding. By combining AI insights with human interpersonal skills, real estate professionals can create more meaningful and successful interactions with potential buyers.

In addition to training, real estate companies need to establish clear guidelines and best practices for the ethical use of humanistic AI. This includes ensuring that data is collected and used responsibly, with a focus on privacy and consent. Companies should also implement measures to address and mitigate potential biases in AI algorithms. Regular audits and updates of AI systems are essential to ensure that they remain fair and accurate.

As humanistic AI continues to evolve, its potential applications in the real estate industry will expand. Future advancements may include even more sophisticated emotional analysis capabilities, such as the ability to detect micro-expressions and body language cues. These developments will further enhance the predictive power of AI, allowing property professionals to gain even deeper insights into the minds of potential buyers.

The integration of humanistic AI into the real estate industry also has the potential to drive significant cultural and operational changes. Traditional real estate practices often prioritize volume over quality, focusing on generating as many leads as possible in the hope that a small percentage will convert. Humanistic AI challenges this approach by emphasizing the importance of understanding and addressing the needs of individual buyers. This shift requires a more empathetic and customer-centric mindset, which can ultimately lead to more meaningful and successful interactions.

Furthermore, the adoption of humanistic AI can lead to more collaborative and transparent relationships between buyers, sellers, and agents. By providing a deeper understanding of the emotional states and motivations of all parties involved, AI can help to build trust and foster open communication. This can create a more positive and supportive environment, ultimately leading to better outcomes for everyone involved.

The future of real estate lies in the integration of advanced technologies, and humanistic AI is at the forefront of this transformation. The challenges faced by real estate developers may be significant, but humanistic AI offers a powerful solution.

CHAPTER SIX

THE RISE OF THE MACHINES
AI-POWERED ROBOT SALES AGENTS

In recent years, the fields of robotics and AI have seen incredible advancements, and their convergence is beginning to reshape various industries. One such industry poised for transformation is real estate, where the concept of AI-powered robot sales agents is rapidly becoming a reality. These advancements are not just technological curiosities but represent a fundamental shift in how sales operations can be conducted, offering significant advantages over traditional human agents.

The idea of robots replacing property professionals in a real estate sales environment may have seemed far-fetched a decade ago, but today it is becoming increasingly feasible. Robots equipped with conversational AI capabilities can interact with clients, provide detailed information about properties, and handle numerous inquiries simultaneously. This technology holds the promise of enhancing the efficiency and effectiveness of real estate sales centers, ultimately transforming the customer experience.

One of the most significant advantages of AI-powered robot sales agents is their access to perfect information. Unlike human agents, who must rely on their memory and notes, robots can instantly access and process vast amounts of data. This includes detailed property information, market trends, legal requirements, and customer preferences. With this comprehensive knowledge, robot agents can provide accurate and consistent information to potential buyers, addressing their queries with precision and confidence. Moreover, robots bring an element of novelty and intrigue that can attract customers to sales centers. The novelty factor alone can be a significant draw, enticing potential buyers to visit and interact with these cutting-edge technologies. This increased foot traffic can lead to more opportunities for sales and engagement. The presence of robots in sales environments also signals to customers that the company is innovative and forward-thinking, which can enhance the brand's reputation and appeal.

Several companies have made remarkable strides in developing humanoid robots capable of engaging in human-like conversations. These robots are designed to mimic human behavior and speech patterns, making interactions feel natural and intuitive. For example, SoftBank Robotics' Pepper robot is one of the most well-known humanoid robots used in various customer service roles, including retail and hospitality. Pepper can recognize faces, understand emotions, and engage in meaningful conversations, making it an ideal candidate for real estate sales.

Another notable example is Hanson Robotics' Sophia, a highly advanced humanoid robot that has garnered international attention for her human-like appearance and conversational abilities. Sophia can hold conversations, express a wide range of emotions, and even remember past interactions. This level of sophistication makes her a powerful tool for engaging with potential buyers, providing personalized experiences, and building trust.

These robots are not just limited to simple interactions. With advancements in AI, they can analyze customer behavior and preferences to tailor their responses and recommendations. For instance, if a customer expresses interest in a particular type of property, the robot can provide detailed information about similar properties, including pricing, location, amenities, and even future market projections. This level of personalized service can enhance the customer experience, making it more likely that they will proceed with a purchase.

The integration of AI with robotics also enables these sales agents to handle complex tasks that would be challenging for humans. For example, they can manage and analyze large datasets to identify trends and insights that can inform sales strategies. They can also automate routine tasks, such as scheduling appointments, sending follow-up emails, and generating reports, freeing up human agents to focus on higher-value activities.

The potential of AI-powered robot sales agents extends beyond customer interactions. These robots can also serve as valuable tools for training and supporting human agents. By observing and learning from the robots' interactions, human agents can improve their own skills and techniques. Additionally, robots can provide real-time feedback and guidance to human agents during sales interactions, helping them navigate complex conversations and address customer concerns more effectively.

The deployment of robot sales agents is not without challenges, however. One of the primary concerns is the initial cost of acquiring and maintaining these advanced technologies. While the long-term benefits and efficiencies may outweigh these costs, the upfront investment can be substantial. Companies must carefully consider the return on investment and develop a clear strategy for integrating robots into their sales operations.

Another challenge is ensuring that these robots can seamlessly interact with diverse customer populations. Different customers have varying levels of comfort and familiarity with technology, and some may prefer human interactions over robotic ones. It is essential for companies to strike the right balance and offer options that cater to different customer preferences. Additionally, continuous improvement and updates to the robots' AI systems are necessary to keep them relevant and effective in an ever-changing market.

Despite these challenges, the potential benefits of AI-powered robot sales agents are too significant to ignore. By leveraging these technologies, real estate companies can enhance their sales operations, improve customer experiences, and gain a competitive edge in the market. As the technology continues to evolve, it is likely that we will see even more sophisticated and capable robots entering the real estate industry.

One of the most promising aspects of AI-powered robots is their ability to learn and adapt over time. Through machine learning algorithms, these robots can continuously improve their interactions and decision-making processes. This means that the more they interact with customers, the better they become at understanding and responding to their needs. This continuous learning loop can lead to increasingly personalized and effective sales interactions, ultimately driving higher conversion rates. In addition to enhancing sales interactions, AI-powered robots can also play a crucial role in data collection and analysis. Every interaction with a customer generates valuable data that can be analyzed to gain insights into customer preferences, market trends, and sales performance.

Robots can collect this data in real-time, providing companies with a wealth of information that can be used to refine sales strategies and make data-driven decisions. This level of insight is invaluable for staying ahead of the competition and adapting to changing market conditions.

The use of AI-powered robots in real estate sales also has the potential to reduce operational costs. By automating routine tasks and streamlining processes, companies can achieve significant efficiencies and reduce the need for a large sales workforce. This can lead to cost savings that can be reinvested in other areas of the business, like marketing, product development, or customer service.

Moreover, the scalability of robot sales agents is a significant advantage. Unlike human agents, who are limited by time and capacity, robots can handle multiple interactions simultaneously and operate 24/7. This means that sales centers can remain open and responsive to customer inquiries at all times, providing a level of service that is difficult to achieve with human agents alone. This scalability is particularly valuable in high-demand markets or during peak sales periods, where the ability to handle a large volume of inquiries can make a significant difference in sales performance.

The rise of AI-powered robot sales agents also has broader implications for the real estate industry as a whole. As more companies adopt these technologies, there will likely be a shift in industry standards and expectations. Customers will come to expect a higher level of service and responsiveness, and companies that fail to keep up with these expectations may find themselves at a competitive disadvantage. This shift could drive further innovation and investment in AI and robotics, leading to even more advanced and capable technologies in the future.

In addition to transforming sales interactions, AI-powered robots can also play a role in property management and maintenance. For example, robots equipped with sensors and cameras can conduct virtual tours of properties, identifying potential issues and reporting them to property managers. This can streamline the inspection process and ensure that properties are well-maintained, ultimately enhancing the value and appeal of the properties being sold. Furthermore, the integration of AI and robotics in real estate is not limited to the sales center.

Smart home technologies, powered by AI, are becoming increasingly popular among buyers. These technologies can automate various aspects of home management, from climate control to security, providing added convenience and efficiency for homeowners. The ability to showcase these smart home features through robot sales agents can further enhance the appeal of properties and demonstrate the benefits of modern technology to potential buyers.

The potential of AI-powered robots to transform the real estate industry is immense, but it is essential to approach this transformation thoughtfully and strategically. Companies must invest in the right technologies, provide adequate training and support for their human agents, and continuously monitor and refine their AI systems to ensure they remain effective and relevant. By doing so, they can harness the power of AI and robotics to drive innovation, enhance customer experiences, and achieve greater success in the market.

The rise of AI-powered robot sales agents represents a significant opportunity for the real estate industry. These technologies offer numerous advantages, including access to perfect information, the ability to handle complex tasks, and the potential to enhance customer experiences.

By leveraging these technologies, real estate companies can improve their sales operations, reduce costs, and gain a competitive edge in the market. While there are challenges to overcome, the potential benefits far outweigh the risks. As AI and robotics continue to evolve, the real estate industry will likely see even more transformative changes in the years to come. The future of real estate sales is bright, and AI-powered robots are poised to play a central role in this exciting transformation.

One of the key areas where AI-powered robots can make a significant impact is in the realm of customer engagement and relationship management. Traditional customer relationship management (CRM) systems are often limited by their reliance on manual data entry and analysis.

AI-powered robots, however, can automate these processes, providing real-time insights and recommendations that enhance the customer experience. For example, robots can track customer interactions, preferences, and feedback, using this data to personalize their interactions and offer tailored recommendations.

This level of personalization can significantly improve customer satisfaction and loyalty, leading to higher conversion rates and repeat business. Moreover, AI-powered robots can enhance the transparency and accountability of real estate transactions. One of the common challenges in real estate is the complexity and opacity of the buying process. Customers often struggle to navigate the various legal, financial, and logistical aspects of purchasing a property.

AI-powered robots can demystify this process by providing clear, accurate, and timely information at every stage of the transaction. For instance, robots can guide customers through the paperwork, explain legal terms, and answer questions about financing options. This level of support can reduce the stress and uncertainty associated with buying a property, making the process more accessible and enjoyable for customers.

Another promising application of AI-powered robots in real estate is in the realm of virtual and augmented reality (VR/AR). These technologies are already being used to create immersive virtual tours of properties, allowing potential buyers to explore homes from the comfort of their own devices.

AI-powered robots can enhance these virtual tours by acting as virtual guides, providing real-time information and answering questions as customers navigate the property. For example, a robot could highlight key features of the home, provide historical and market data, and even suggest design ideas based on the buyer's preferences. This interactive and immersive experience can make virtual tours more engaging and informative, increasing the likelihood of a sale.

The integration of AI-powered robots with smart home technologies also presents exciting possibilities. As more homes become equipped with smart devices, robots can act as central hubs that control and manage these systems. For example, a robot could adjust the lighting, temperature, and security settings based on the homeowner's preferences and routines.

This level of automation and customization can enhance the comfort and convenience of living in a smart home, making it a more attractive option for buyers. Additionally, robots can provide real-time monitoring and alerts, ensuring that the home remains secure and efficient at all times.

In addition to enhancing the buying process, AI-powered robots can also play a crucial role in the post-purchase phase. After a property is sold, robots can continue to engage with customers, providing ongoing support and assistance. For example, a robot could help new homeowners settle in by providing information about the local area, such as nearby schools, shops, and services.

It could also offer maintenance tips and reminders, ensuring that the property remains in good condition. This level of post-purchase support can strengthen the relationship between the real estate company and the customer, increasing the likelihood of referrals and repeat business.

The potential applications of AI-powered robots in real estate are vast, and the benefits they offer are significant. However, it is important for companies to approach this technology with a clear strategy and vision. The successful integration of robots into the sales process requires careful planning, investment, and training.

Companies must ensure that their robots are equipped with the latest AI technologies, capable of delivering accurate and relevant information, and able to interact seamlessly with customers. They must also provide ongoing training and support for their human agents, ensuring that they can work effectively alongside their robotic counterparts.

Companies must also address the ethical and social implications of using AI-powered robots in real estate. The collection and use of personal data must be handled responsibly, with a focus on privacy and consent. Companies must be transparent about how data is collected, stored, and used, and they must ensure that their AI systems are free from bias and discrimination. By addressing these ethical considerations, companies can build trust with their customers and create a more inclusive and equitable real estate market.

The rise of AI-powered robot sales agents represents a significant opportunity for the real estate industry. By leveraging these new technologies, real estate industry. By leveraging these new technologies, real estate companies can improve their sales operations, reduce costs, and gain a competitive edge in the market. While there are challenges to overcome, the potential benefits far outweigh the risks.

CHAPTER SEVEN

THE FUTURE IS D2C
SELLING PROPERTY DEVELOPER 2 CONSUMER

The real estate industry is on the cusp of a significant transformation driven by the emergence of advanced AI technologies. As these technologies continue to evolve, the role of traditional estate agents is set to diminish, paving the way for a future where direct-to-consumer (D2C) sales become the norm.

For decades, real estate developers have relied heavily on estate agents and channel partners to market and sell their properties. However, AI is reversing this trend by equipping developers with the tools and capabilities needed to reach and service customers directly. This shift promises to disrupt the market, offering developers greater control over the sales process, improved efficiency, and significant cost savings.

The traditional model of property sales involves multiple intermediaries, each adding layers of complexity and cost to the process. Estate agents and channel partners play crucial roles in connecting developers with potential buyers, but their involvement also means that developers must share a portion of their profits in the form of commissions. Additionally, the reliance on intermediaries can lead to inefficiencies, miscommunications, and delays, ultimately affecting the overall customer experience.

AI technologies are changing the game by providing developers with powerful prospecting tools, enabling them to identify and market to the right customers with unprecedented precision. Through advanced data analytics and machine learning algorithms, AI can analyze vast amounts of data to identify potential buyers based on their preferences, behaviors, and past interactions. This level of targeting ensures that marketing efforts are directed towards individuals who are most likely to be interested in the properties being offered, thereby increasing the likelihood of successful sales.

Moreover, AI-powered marketing platforms can automate and optimize various aspects of the marketing process. From crafting personalized messages to managing multi-channel campaigns, AI can handle tasks that would traditionally require significant time and effort from human marketers. This automation not only improves efficiency but also allows developers to scale their marketing efforts, reaching a larger audience without an increase in resources.

One of the key advantages of AI in the D2C model is its ability to provide perfect information to both developers and consumers. In the traditional model, information asymmetry often exists, with buyers relying on agents to provide them with accurate and complete information about properties. AI eliminates this asymmetry by making detailed property information readily available to buyers. Virtual tours, augmented reality (AR) applications, and interactive property maps powered by AI can provide potential buyers with a comprehensive understanding of the properties they are interested in, without the need for physical visits.

Additionally, AI can enhance the customer service experience by providing instant, accurate responses to inquiries. AI-powered chatbots and virtual assistants can handle a wide range of customer interactions, like answering basic questions, scheduling viewings and providing detailed property information.

These tools can operate 24/7, ensuring that potential buyers receive timely responses regardless of when they make inquiries. This level of responsiveness can significantly improve the customer experience, making it more likely that buyers will proceed with a purchase.

Robotics, as previously discussed, also plays a crucial role in the D2C model by augmenting the capabilities of AI. Humanoid robots equipped with advanced conversational AI can interact with customers in sales centers, providing them with personalized assistance and information. These robots can handle multiple customers simultaneously, ensuring that everyone receives the attention they need. The novelty factor of interacting with a robot can also draw more customers to sales centers, increasing foot traffic and the potential for sales.

The shift to a D2C model offers numerous benefits for real estate developers. One of the most significant advantages is the potential for cost savings. By eliminating the need for intermediaries, developers can retain a larger portion of their profits. The cost savings from reduced commission payments can be substantial, especially for large-scale projects. These savings can be reinvested in other areas of the business, such as marketing, product development, or enhancing the customer experience.

Furthermore, the D2C model allows developers to have greater control over the sales process. In the traditional model, developers often rely on agents to represent their interests and manage customer interactions. While many agents are highly skilled and professional, there is always a risk of miscommunication or misalignment of priorities.

By taking control of the sales process, developers can ensure that their brand and message are consistently communicated to potential buyers. This direct engagement also allows developers to gather valuable feedback from customers, which can be used to improve future projects and marketing strategies.

The efficiency gains from using AI and robotics in the sales process are another significant advantage. Traditional sales processes can be time-consuming and labor-intensive, with agents spending a significant amount of time on tasks such as scheduling viewings, following up with leads, and managing paperwork. AI can automate many of these tasks, freeing up human resources to focus on more strategic activities. For example, AI can automatically schedule viewings based on the availability of both the customer and the property, send follow-up emails and reminders, and even generate contracts and other documents.

The scalability of the D2C model is another critical benefit. Traditional sales models are often limited by the availability and capacity of human agents. In contrast, AI-powered systems can handle an unlimited number of interactions simultaneously, ensuring that all potential buyers receive timely and personalized attention.

This scalability is particularly valuable for large-scale projects or during peak sales periods when demand is high. By leveraging AI and robotics, developers can manage a large volume of inquiries and interactions without compromising on the quality of customer service.

The transition to a D2C model is not without its challenges. One of the primary concerns is the initial investment required to develop and implement AI and robotic systems. While the long-term benefits and cost savings are significant, the upfront costs can be substantial. Developers need to carefully assess their financial situation and develop a clear strategy for integrating these technologies into their operations. This may involve partnering with technology providers, investing in training and development for staff, and gradually phasing in AI and robotics over time.

Another challenge is ensuring that AI and robotic systems can seamlessly integrate with existing processes and systems. Many real estate developers have established ways of working and may be resistant to change. It is essential to ensure that the transition to a D2C model is as smooth as possible, with minimal disruption to ongoing operations. This may involve conducting pilot projects to test the new technologies, gathering feedback from staff and customers, and making adjustments as needed.

Despite these challenges, the potential benefits of the D2C model are too significant to ignore. The real estate industry is ripe for disruption, and developers who embrace AI and robotics will be well-positioned to lead this transformation. By leveraging these technologies, developers can improve efficiency, reduce costs, and enhance the customer experience. The result is a streamlined and profitable sales process that benefits developers and buyers.

As AI and robotics continue to evolve, the capabilities of these technologies will only improve. Future advancements may include even more sophisticated AI algorithms, more intuitive and responsive robots, and enhanced data analytics capabilities. These developments will further enhance the effectiveness of the D2C model, making it an increasingly attractive option for real estate developers.

The rise of the D2C model also has broader implications for the real estate industry. As more developers adopt this approach, traditional estate agents may need to adapt to stay relevant. This could involve offering more specialized services, focusing on niche markets, or partnering with developers to provide complementary support. The role of estate agents is likely to evolve, with a greater greater emphasis on providing high-value, personalized services that cannot be easily automated.

In addition to transforming the sales process, the D2C model can also drive innovation in other areas of real estate. For example, developers can use the data collected through AI systems to gain deeper insights into buyer preferences and market trends. This information can inform the design and development of new projects, ensuring that they meet the needs and expectations of buyers. Developers can also use AI to optimize pricing strategies, ensuring that properties are competitively priced and aligned with market conditions.

The shift to a D2C model also has the potential to enhance the transparency and accountability of real estate transactions. By providing buyers with direct access to information and eliminating intermediaries, developers can create a more open and straightforward buying process. This can build trust and confidence among buyers, making them more likely to proceed with a purchase.

The emergence of AI technologies is driving a significant shift in the real estate industry, with the rise of the D2C model offering developers a powerful new way to reach and service customers. By leveraging AI and robotics, developers can take control of the sales process, improve efficiency, reduce costs, and enhance the customer experience. While there are challenges to overcome, the potential benefits of the D2C model are substantial. As AI and robotics continue to evolve, the real estate industry will likely see even more transformative changes in the years to come. The future of real estate sales is direct-to-consumer, and developers who embrace this model will be well-positioned to lead the industry into a new era of innovation and growth.

Expanding on this transformation, consider the implications of enhanced data privacy and security measures that AI technologies bring to the table. In traditional real estate transactions, sensitive information is often shared across multiple parties, increasing the risk of data breaches and fraud. AI systems, however, can incorporate advanced encryption and security protocols to protect customer data. This ensures that personal and financial information remains secure throughout the transaction process, fostering greater trust and confidence among buyers.

Moreover, the use of AI and robotics can lead to more environmentally sustainable practices in real estate. AI can optimize energy usage in sales centers and smart homes, reducing the carbon footprint associated with property transactions. Robots can perform maintenance and inspections with greater efficiency, identifying areas where energy can be saved. This focus on sustainability not only benefits the environment but also appeals to eco-conscious consumers, further enhancing the attractiveness of the D2C model.

Another critical aspect of the D2C model is the potential for enhanced customer engagement and loyalty. AI-driven customer relationship management (CRM) systems can track and analyze every interaction a buyer has with a developer, providing personalized recommendations and follow-ups. This level of personalized attention can lead to higher customer satisfaction and loyalty, encouraging repeat business and referrals. For instance, after a purchase, AI can continue to engage with the buyer, offering maintenance tips, updates on the property's value, and information about new developments, thereby maintaining a long-term relationship.

The D2C model also opens up new avenues for innovative marketing strategies. Developers can leverage AI to create immersive virtual reality (VR) and augmented reality (AR) experiences that allow buyers to explore properties in a highly engaging and interactive manner. These technologies can bring properties to life, offering virtual tours that showcase the finer details of a home, its surroundings, and even future development plans. This immersive experience can significantly enhance the decision-making process, making it easier for buyers to visualize themselves in the property and commit to a purchase.

Furthermore, AI can facilitate more effective social media marketing campaigns. By analyzing social media trends and user behavior, AI can help developers craft targeted ads that resonate with specific demographics. Social media platforms can also serve as powerful tools for gathering feedback and insights from potential buyers, allowing developers to refine their offerings and marketing strategies continually.

In terms of operational efficiency, AI can streamline the entire sales process from lead generation to closing the deal. For example, AI-powered systems can automatically qualify leads based on predefined criteria, ensuring that sales teams focus on the most promising prospects. These systems can also track the progress of each lead through the sales funnel, providing real-time updates and analytics that help sales teams optimize their efforts.

Robotic process automation (RPA) is another aspect that can be integrated into the D2C model. RPA can handle repetitive administrative tasks such as document processing, contract management, and compliance checks. By automating these tasks, developers can reduce the risk of errors, ensure compliance with regulatory requirements, and free up human resources to focus on strategic initiatives.

The scalability of AI and robotic systems also means that developers can efficiently manage large portfolios of properties. Whether it's a single residential building or a sprawling commercial complex, these technologies can handle the complexities involved in managing multiple properties simultaneously. This capability is particularly beneficial for developers looking to expand their operations into new markets or regions.

Looking ahead, the continued advancement of AI promises even more exciting possibilities for the D2C model. The transition to a D2C model represents not just a technological evolution but a fundamental transformation in the way real estate business is conducted.

CHAPTER EIGHT

RISK, FEAR & ANXIETY
OVERCOMING THE PITFALLS OF PROJECT LAUNCHES

The real estate business is inherently high-stakes, involving substantial sums of money and significant risks. The scale of these financial transactions is magnified in the real estate development sector, where developers deploy vast amounts of capital to acquire land, construct properties, and eventually launch projects for sale.

The pressure to sell large volumes of real estate quickly to recoup investments and turn profits is immense. This high-pressure environment creates stress and anxiety for developers, who must navigate numerous challenges, from marketing and sales to customer management and financial risk mitigation.

One of the primary challenges in real estate development is the need to sell a substantial number of properties in a short time frame. The success of a project often hinges on the developer's ability to generate significant sales quickly, which is crucial for maintaining cash flow and ensuring the financial viability.

This urgency can lead to high stress levels as developers scramble to implement effective marketing strategies, attract potential buyers, and close deals. Moreover, managing a large number of customers, each with their anxieties and concerns, adds another layer of complexity to the process.

AI technologies offer a transformative solution to these challenges, providing developers with tools to enhance their sales and marketing efforts, improve customer management, and ultimately reduce the risks and anxieties associated with project launches. By leveraging advanced AI capabilities, developers can approach project launches with greater confidence and efficiency.

AI-based sales and marketing tools can significantly improve the speed and effectiveness of property sales. These tools utilize advanced data analytics and machine learning algorithms to identify and target potential buyers with precision. By analyzing vast amounts of data, AI can generate insights into buyer behavior, preferences, and market trends, enabling developers to craft highly targeted marketing campaigns. This level of targeting ensures that marketing efforts reach the right audience, increasing the likelihood of successful sales.

For instance, AI can analyze data from various sources, such as social media, online searches, and past buying behaviors, to create detailed profiles of potential buyers. These profiles can then be used to deliver personalized marketing messages that resonate with individual buyers, making them more likely to engage with the developer and consider purchasing a property.

This targeted approach is far more efficient than traditional marketing methods, which often rely on broad, generic messages that may not effectively capture the attention of potential buyers.

In addition to enhancing targeting, AI can also automate and optimize various aspects of the marketing process. For example, AI-powered platforms can manage multi-channel marketing campaigns, ensuring consistent messaging across different platforms, such as social media, email, and search engines. These platforms can also track the performance of marketing campaigns in real-time, providing developers with insights into what is working and what is not. This real-time feedback allows developers to adjust their strategies on the fly, optimizing their marketing efforts for maximum impact.

One of the most significant stress points for real estate developers is the sheer volume of follow-up required to convert leads into sales. Following up with potential buyers, answering their questions, and addressing their concerns can be incredibly time-consuming, especially when dealing with large numbers of leads. This is where AI's automation capabilities come into play. AI-powered systems can handle a vast number of follow-up tasks, ensuring that no lead is overlooked and that every potential buyer receives timely and personalized attention.

For example, AI-powered chatbots and virtual assistants can handle initial inquiries from potential buyers, providing instant responses to common questions and guiding them through the early stages of the sales process.

These tools can also schedule follow-up appointments, send reminders, and provide detailed property information, freeing up human agents to focus on more complex tasks. Furthermore, some of the latest AI technologies are capable of making thousands of smart calls every hour, far exceeding the capacity of traditional call centers. This capability ensures that potential buyers receive the information and follow-up they need promptly, improving their overall experience and increasing the likelihood of a sale.

The ability of AI to manage large-scale sales and marketing efforts, automate follow-up processes, and provide accurate information dramatically reduces the risk for real estate developers. By streamlining these critical aspects of the sales process, AI helps developers overcome the fear and anxiety associated with project launches. Developers can approach launches with greater confidence, knowing that they have the tools to generate sales quickly and efficiently.

In addition to reducing the stress and anxiety for developers, AI also addresses the concerns of potential buyers. Purchasing real estate is a significant financial commitment, and buyers often experience anxiety and uncertainty throughout the process. AI can help alleviate these concerns by providing buyers with accurate, comprehensive information about properties and the buying process.

For instance, AI-powered virtual tours and augmented reality (AR) applications can provide potential buyers with immersive, interactive experiences that allow them to explore properties in detail from the comfort of their own homes. These technologies can showcase every aspect of a property, from room layouts and finishes to neighborhood amenities and future development plans. By providing a clear and detailed view of what they are purchasing, these tools help reduce buyer anxiety and build confidence in their decision-making.

Moreover, AI can enhance transparency in the buying process by providing real-time updates and insights. Potential buyers can receive instant notifications about about the status of their inquiries, the progress of their applications, and any changes to property availability or pricing. This level of transparency helps build trust between developers and buyers, further reducing anxiety and fostering a positive buying experience.

AI's ability to personalize interactions also plays a crucial role in addressing buyer concerns. By analyzing data on buyer preferences and behaviors, AI can tailor its interactions to meet the specific needs and interests of each buyer. For example, if a buyer expresses interest in properties with specific features, such as energy-efficient appliances or proximity to schools, AI can prioritize showing properties that match these criteria. This personalized approach ensures that buyers feel understood and valued, enhancing their overall experience and increasing their likelihood of proceeding with a purchase.

The benefits of AI extend beyond the initial sales process. Once a property is sold, AI can continue to support both developers and buyers through the post-sale phase. For developers, AI can manage post-sale follow-up tasks, such as coordinating move-in schedules, handling customer service inquiries, and managing maintenance requests. This level of support ensures that buyers remain satisfied and engaged even after the sale is completed, fostering long-term relationships and encouraging referrals.

For buyers, AI can provide ongoing assistance with property management and maintenance. AI-powered home management systems can monitor and control various aspects of the property, such as heating, cooling, lighting, and security. These systems can provide maintenance reminders and alerts, ensuring that the property remains in optimal condition. This level of support helps buyers feel secure in their purchase, reducing the stress associated with property ownership.

The integration of AI into real estate development also has significant implications for risk management. One of the primary risks in real estate development is market volatility, which can impact property values and buyer demand. AI's advanced data analytics capabilities can help developers mitigate this risk by providing accurate market forecasts and identifying emerging trends. By analyzing historical data, current market conditions, and economic indicators,

AI can generate predictive models that help developers make informed decisions about when and where to launch projects. For example, AI can analyze factors such as population growth, employment rates, and infrastructure developments to identify areas with high potential for future demand. This information allows developers to strategically plan their projects, ensuring that they are launched in markets with strong growth prospects. Additionally, AI can provide insights into pricing strategies, helping developers set competitive prices that attract buyers while maximizing profitability.

AI can also assist developers in managing financial risk by optimizing cash flow and budgeting. AI-powered financial management tools can analyze project expenses, revenues, and timelines to identify potential cash flow issues and recommend corrective actions. These tools can also provide real-time financial reports and forecasts, enabling developers to monitor the financial health of their projects and make data-driven decisions.

Furthermore, AI can enhance compliance and regulatory risk management by automating the monitoring and reporting of compliance requirements. Real estate development involves navigating a complex web of regulations and standards, and non-compliance can result in costly penalties and delays. AI-powered compliance tools can track regulatory changes, monitor compliance activities, and generate reports, ensuring that developers remain in compliance with all relevant requirements. This level of automation reduces the risk of non-compliance and helps developers avoid costly legal issues.

The real estate development business is fraught with risks, challenges, and stress. However, the emergence of advanced AI technologies offers a transformative solution that can help developers overcome these pitfalls.

By leveraging AI for sales and marketing, customer management, and risk mitigation, developers can approach project launches with greater confidence and efficiency. The future of real estate development lies in the strategic integration of AI technologies. By overcoming the pitfalls of project launches with the power of AI, developers can unlock new opportunities for growth and success in the competitive real estate market.

CHAPTER NINE

THE GLOBAL SUPER BUYER
USING AI TO FIND CUSTOMERS ANYWHERE

In previous decades, real estate was primarily a local game. Development projects were built within regions and typically marketed to potential customers within those same regions. However, recent trends in globalization have fundamentally transformed the real estate landscape, making it a "glocal" industry—both global and local. The rise of mobile capital and the ease of buying property across boundaries, regions, and continents have redefined how developers approach marketing and sales.

Globalization has led to an increase in the number of global cities—cities that are significant nodes in the global economic system. These cities, numbering around 25, have become hubs where buyers can be sourced for international projects and markets. This shift from local to global marketing presents both opportunities and challenges for real estate developers.

Traditional sales and marketing approaches are often ill-equipped to handle the scale and complexity of targeting a global audience. However, with the advent of AI tools, developers can now prospect and find buyers across the world with unprecedented efficiency and accuracy.

AI technologies have revolutionized the way real estate developers can identify and engage potential buyers on a global scale. One of the most significant advantages of AI is its ability to analyze vast amounts of data from many sources to identify potential buyers who are most likely to be interested in a particular property. This data-driven approach to prospecting allows developers to extend their reach beyond local markets and tap into a global pool of potential buyers.

For example, AI can analyze data from social media, online searches, and real estate platforms to identify individuals who have shown interest in purchasing property in specific regions or cities. By leveraging machine learning algorithms, AI can identify patterns and trends that indicate a high likelihood of purchase, allowing developers to target these individuals with tailored marketing messages. This level of precision is impossible to achieve with traditional marketing methods, which often rely on broad and generic campaigns that may not resonate with a global audience.

In addition to identifying potential buyers, AI can also automate and optimize the follow-up and engagement process. Real estate transactions often involve multiple touchpoints and follow-ups, which can be time-consuming and challenging to manage, especially when dealing with a global audience. AI-powered tools can handle these tasks with ease, ensuring that potential buyers receive timely and personalized responses regardless of their location.

For instance, AI-powered chatbots and virtual assistants can manage initial inquiries from potential buyers, providing instant responses to common questions and guiding them through the early stages of the sales process. These tools can also schedule follow-up appointments, send reminders, and provide detailed property information, freeing up human agents to focus on more complex tasks. Furthermore, AI systems can make thousands of smart calls every hour, far exceeding the capacity of traditional call centers. This capability ensures that potential buyers receive the information and follow-up they need promptly, improving their overall experience and increasing the likelihood of a sale.

One of the challenges of targeting a global audience is the need to manage language barriers and time zone differences. Real-time language translation and time zone management are essential for effective communication and engagement with potential buyers from different parts of the world. AI technologies have made significant strides in these areas, providing solutions that facilitate seamless communication across languages and time zones.

AI-powered translation tools can provide real-time language translation, which enable developers to communicate with potential buyers in their preferred language. These tools can translate text, speech, and even live conversations, ensuring that language barriers do not hinder the sales process. This capability is particularly valuable for developers targeting buyers in non-English-speaking regions, as it allows them to provide personalized and responsive communication that builds trust and confidence.

Time zone management is another critical aspect of engaging a global audience. AI-powered scheduling tools can automatically adjust for time zone differences, ensuring that appointments and follow-ups are scheduled at convenient times for both parties. These tools can also send reminders and notifications based on the recipient's local time, ensuring that potential buyers receive timely updates regardless of their location. This level of automation and precision helps streamline the sales process and reduces the risk of missed opportunities due to time zone discrepancies.

The ability of AI to prospect, engage, and manage a global audience has significant implications for real estate developers. By leveraging AI, developers can expand their reach beyond local markets and tap into a global pool of potential buyers. This global approach to marketing and sales not only increases the likelihood of successful transactions but also enhances the overall efficiency and effectiveness of the sales process.

Furthermore, AI's data-driven approach allows developers to gain deeper insights into buyer behavior and preferences. By analyzing data from multiple sources, AI can identify trends and patterns that provide valuable insights into what drives buyer decisions.

This information can inform marketing strategies, helping developers craft messages that resonate with their target audience. For example, AI can identify the types of properties that are most popular among buyers from specific regions, allowing developers to tailor their offerings to meet these preferences.

The rise of the global super buyer also has implications for the types of properties that developers choose to build. Understanding the preferences and behaviors of a global audience can help developers identify new opportunities and trends in the market. For instance, AI may reveal a growing interest in eco-friendly and sustainable properties among buyers from certain regions.

Developers can use this information to design and build properties that cater to these preferences, increasing their appeal to a global audience.

The ability to target a global audience also opens up new opportunities for collaboration and partnerships. Developers can leverage their AI-powered insights to form strategic partnerships with international real estate agencies, marketing firms, and other stakeholders. These partnerships can help developers expand their reach and tap into new markets, further enhancing their ability to attract global buyers.

One of the most exciting aspects of using AI to target global buyers is the potential for innovation in marketing and sales strategies. AI-powered tools can create immersive and interactive experiences that engage potential buyers in new and exciting ways. For example, virtual reality (VR) and augmented reality (AR) technologies can provide potential buyers with immersive property tours, allowing them to explore properties from the comfort of their own homes. These technologies can showcase every aspect of a property, from room layouts and finishes to neighborhood amenities and future development plans. By providing a clear and detailed view of what they are purchasing, these tools help reduce buyer anxiety and build confidence in their decision-making.

In addition to VR and AR, AI can also enhance other aspects of the marketing process, such as content creation and distribution. AI-powered tools can generate personalized content that resonates with individual buyers, from targeted email campaigns to social media posts. These tools can also optimize the timing and distribution of content, ensuring that it reaches potential buyers when they are most likely to engage. This level of personalization and optimization can significantly improve the effectiveness of marketing campaigns, increasing the likelihood of successful sales.

The use of AI to target global buyers also has significant implications for the overall efficiency and cost-effectiveness of the sales process. Traditional marketing and sales approaches can be expensive and time-consuming, especially when targeting a global audience.

AI-powered tools can streamline these processes, reducing the time and resources required to identify, engage, and convert potential buyers. This increased efficiency can result in significant cost savings for developers, allowing them to allocate more resources to other areas of their business, such as product development and customer service.

Moreover, the ability to target a global audience can help developers mitigate the risks associated with market fluctuations and economic uncertainties. By diversifying their buyer base, developers can reduce their reliance on any single market, spreading their risk across multiple regions and countries. This diversification can provide a buffer against economic downturns and market volatility, ensuring more stable and predictable sales outcomes.

The rise of the global super buyer represents a significant shift in the real estate industry, driven by the power of AI technologies. By leveraging AI for prospecting, engagement, and management, developers can expand their reach beyond local markets and tap into a vast pool of potential buyers from around the world.

The future of real estate is glocal, and developers who embrace the power of AI to target global buyers will be well-positioned to lead the industry into a new era of growth and success.

CHAPTER TEN

THE UNSTOPPABLE MARCH OF AI
THE FUTURE IS HERE... NOW

As we draw this exploration of AI in the real estate industry to a close, it's important to reflect on the profound changes already underway and the even more transformative shifts on the horizon. The technologies we've discussed throughout this book—AI-powered sales agents, humanistic AI, global prospecting tools, direct-to-consumer models, and more—are not speculative concepts waiting to be realized in some distant future.

They are here now, actively reshaping the real estate landscape. The next 1,000 days will likely see these advancements accelerate, driving a massive transformation that will redefine how real estate is marketed, sold and managed.

In previous chapters, we've delved into how AI is revolutionizing various aspects of real estate. We've seen how AI-powered robots are beginning to replace human agents in sales centers, offering precise, data-driven interactions and handling thousands of inquiries simultaneously.

Companies like SoftBank Robotics and Hanson Robotics have developed sophisticated humanoid robots like Pepper and Sophia, capable of engaging with customers, understanding their needs, and providing detailed property information. These robots are not just novelties; they represent the future of customer engagement, offering reliability, consistency, and efficiency that human agents simply cannot match.

We also explored the concept of humanistic AI, which uses advanced algorithms to understand and predict human emotions and behaviors. This technology enables real estate professionals to gauge the interest levels of potential buyers, prioritize high-potential leads, and tailor their sales approaches accordingly. By analyzing voice samples or written texts, humanistic AI can provide insights into a buyer's personality and preferences, allowing for highly personalized interactions. This level of personalization was previously unimaginable but is now becoming a standard practice in the industry.

The shift from local to global marketing has been another significant theme. AI's ability to analyze vast amounts of data and identify potential buyers worldwide is breaking down geographical barriers. Real estate developers can now target buyers in global cities, tailoring their marketing efforts to suit diverse preferences and behaviors. Tools like AI-powered translation and time zone management ensure seamless communication, making it easier to engage with buyers across different regions. This global approach is not only expanding market reach but also diversifying risks and stabilizing sales outcomes.

The direct-to-consumer (D2C) model, empowered by AI, is another game-changer. By eliminating intermediaries, developers can take control of the entire sales process, from prospecting to closing deals. AI-driven marketing platforms, CRM systems, and automated follow-up tools are making this model highly efficient and effective. The cost savings from reduced commission payments and the ability to maintain direct relationships with buyers are compelling advantages that are driving the adoption of the D2C model.

One of the most exciting aspects of AI in real estate is its potential to enhance the buyer experience. Virtual reality (VR) and augmented reality (AR) technologies are providing immersive property tours that allow buyers to explore properties in detail from anywhere in the world. These technologies offer a level of engagement and transparency that traditional methods cannot match. Buyers can visualize themselves in the property, understand its features and layout, and make informed decisions with greater confidence.

The impact of AI on real estate goes beyond sales and marketing. AI-driven data analytics is providing developers with deeper insights into market trends, buyer behaviors, and property performance. These insights are informing strategic decisions, from project design and development to pricing and marketing strategies. By leveraging AI, developers can stay ahead of market trends, identify new opportunities, and mitigate risks more effectively.

The integration of AI with other advanced technologies like blockchain and the Internet of Things (IoT) is further enhancing its capabilities. Blockchain technology offers greater transparency and security in real estate transactions, while IoT devices provide real-time data on property conditions and performance. Together, these technologies are creating a more interconnected and efficient real estate ecosystem.

Despite the remarkable advancements we've discussed, it's important to recognize that we are still in the early stages of this transformation. The next 1,000 days will likely see rapid developments in AI technologies, driving even greater changes in the real estate industry. Enhanced personalization will become the norm as AI grows more sophisticated, predicting buyer preferences with increasing accuracy. This will enable developers to create highly targeted marketing and sales strategies, improving engagement and conversion rates.

Greater automation will free up human agents to focus on high-value activities. AI-powered systems will handle everything from lead generation and follow-up to contract management and compliance checks. This will increase efficiency and reduce the potential for human error, streamlining operations and cutting costs.

The integration of AI with smart home technologies will provide buyers with added convenience and efficiency. AI-powered home management systems will monitor and control aspects of the property, from energy usage to security, to enhance the living experience and make smart homes more attractive to buyers.

The ability to target global buyers will become even more crucial as markets continue to interconnect. AI-driven translation and time zone management tools will facilitate seamless communication, making it easier to engage with buyers worldwide. This will allow developers to expand their reach and tap into new markets, driving sales and growth.

AI will also play a key role in promoting sustainable practices in real estate. From optimizing energy usage in smart homes to identifying eco-friendly building materials, AI will help developers meet the growing demand for sustainable properties. This focus on sustainability will not only benefit the environment but also appeal to eco-conscious buyers, increasing the attractiveness of green properties.

Enhanced security and privacy measures will be a priority as AI technologies incorporate advanced encryption and security protocols to protect customer data. This will ensure that personal and financial information remains secure throughout the transaction process, fostering greater trust and confidence among buyers. Greater transparency in real estate transactions will be achieved through AI-driven analytics and blockchain technology.

Buyers will have access to real-time information on property conditions, market trends, and transaction history, making the process more transparent and trustworthy. This will reduce the potential for fraud and disputes, ensuring smoother and more reliable transactions.

Increased collaboration between developers, real estate agents, and other stakeholders will be facilitated by AI. By providing valuable insights and streamlining communication, AI will help create a more cohesive and efficient real estate ecosystem. This will enable stakeholders to work together more effectively, driving innovation and improving outcomes. The rise of AI will drive the emergence of new business models in real estate. From AI-powered real estate platforms to automated property management services, the industry will continue to evolve in response to technological advancements. These new models will create opportunities for innovation, reshaping real estate.

As we look ahead, it's clear that the future of real estate is being shaped by the unstoppable march of AI. The technologies we've discussed are not just futuristic concepts—they are here now, actively transforming the industry. For those who believe that these advancements are far off, it's time to recognize that the future is already upon us. The real estate industry is on the brink of a massive transformation, and those who embrace AI will lead the way.

The journey we've explored in this book highlights the incredible potential of AI in real estate. From AI-powered sales agents and humanistic AI to global prospecting tools and the direct-to-consumer model, the applications of AI are vast and varied. These technologies are enhancing efficiency, improving the buyer experience in ways that were previously unimaginable.

As we move forward, the next 1,000 days will be crucial in shaping the future of real estate. The advancements in AI will continue to accelerate, bringing about a new era of growth, innovation, and success for those who are ready to embrace the change. The future is here, and it is unstoppable.

The rise of AI in real estate is not just a technological revolution; it is a paradigm shift that redefines the roles of human agents and robots. By working together, humans and robots can create a more efficient, transparent, and customer-centric real estate market. As we embrace this new era, the possibilities for innovation and growth are limitless. The future is now, and those who adapt to this new reality will lead the way in shaping the future of real estate sales.

Imagine a scenario where a potential buyer in Tokyo can explore a new development in New York City through an immersive VR tour, guided by an AI-powered virtual assistant that answers their questions in real-time and in their native language. Meanwhile, a developer in London uses AI-driven analytics to identify emerging market trends in Dubai, adjusting their marketing strategies accordingly to attract buyers from that region. These scenarios are not science fiction—they are becoming a reality as AI continues to advance and integrate into every aspect of the real estate industry.

Consider the case of a real estate firm that implemented AI-powered chatbots to handle customer inquiries. Initially skeptical, the firm soon realized that these chatbots could handle thousands of inquiries simultaneously, providing instant responses and significantly reducing the workload for human agents. The chatbots were also able to gather valuable data on customer preferences and behaviors, which the firm used to refine its marketing strategies and improve its overall customer service. This real-world example demonstrates the tangible benefits of embracing AI in real estate.

The unstoppable march of AI is also fostering greater innovation in property management. AI-powered systems can monitor the condition of properties in real-time, identifying maintenance issues before they become major problems. These systems can also optimize energy usage, ensuring that properties are both cost-effective and environmentally friendly. By providing real-time data and insights, AI is helping property managers make more informed decisions and enhance the value of their assets.

Furthermore, AI is playing a crucial role in enhancing security and privacy in real estate transactions. Blockchain technology, combined with AI-driven analytics, is providing greater transparency and security, ensuring that all transactions are recorded immutably and can be easily verified. This reduces the risk of fraud and builds trust among buyers and sellers, making the transaction process smoother and more reliable.

As AI continues to evolve, we can expect to see even more innovative applications in real estate. For instance, AI could be used to create predictive models that forecast future market trends with unprecedented accuracy. These models could help developers anticipate changes in buyer preferences and market conditions, allowing them to stay ahead of the competition and capitalize on new opportunities. AI could also be used to develop new financing models that make property ownership more accessible and affordable, further democratizing the real estate market.

The potential of AI in real estate is truly limitless, and the pace of change is accelerating. The next 1,000 days will see rapid advancements in AI technologies, driving further transformation in the industry. Developers, real estate agents, and other stakeholders who embrace these changes will be well-positioned to thrive in this new era. The future is here, and it is unstoppable.

The unstoppable march of AI is transforming the real estate industry in profound and exciting ways. The technologies we've discussed throughout this book are not just futuristic concepts—they are here now, actively reshaping the industry. From AI-powered sales agents and humanistic AI to global prospecting tools and the direct-to-consumer model, the applications of AI are vast and varied. These technologies are enhancing efficiency, improving the buyer experience, and driving innovation in ways that were previously unimaginable.

As we move forward, the next 1,000 days will be crucial in shaping the future of real estate. The advancements in AI will continue to accelerate, bringing about a new era of growth, innovation, and success for those who are ready to embrace the change. The future is here, and it is unstoppable. The rise of AI in real estate is not just a technological revolution; it is a paradigm shift that redefines the roles of human agents and robots. By working together, humans and robots can create a more efficient, transparent, and customer-centric real estate market.

As we embrace this new era, the possibilities for innovation and growth are limitless. The future is now, and those who adapt to this new reality will lead the way in shaping the future of real estate sales.

By focusing on the here and now, we've seen that AI technologies are actively transforming the real estate industry, and their impact will only grow in the coming years. Embracing these technologies today means being prepared for the opportunities and challenges of tomorrow.

The future of real estate is here, and it is driven by the unstoppable march of AI. Those who recognize and adapt to this new reality will be the leaders of the industry, driving innovation, growth, and success in ways that were previously unimaginable.

AFTERWORD

As we reach the end of this book, I find myself reflecting on the remarkable journey we've taken together through the pages of this book. The real estate industry, once rooted in traditional practices and often slow to adapt, is now on the cusp of a technological transformation that promises to redefine every aspect of how we buy, sell, and manage properties. This revolution is driven by the relentless march of artificial intelligence, and its impact is already being felt across the globe.

Writing this book has been an eye-opening experience. I've had the privilege of speaking with visionaries and experts who are at the forefront of integrating AI into real estate. Their insights and experiences have underscored the immense potential of these technologies and the profound changes they are bringing about. What has struck me most is the sheer pace of innovation and the tangible benefits that AI is delivering to developers, agents, and buyers alike.

As you close this book, I hope you feel as inspired and excited about the future as I do. The advancements we've discussed are not distant dreams; they are present realities that are reshaping our industry today. Whether you're a seasoned real estate professional, an investor, or simply someone with an interest in the intersection of technology and property, there's no doubt that AI will play a significant role in your future.

Embracing this change requires an open mind and a willingness to adapt. It means rethinking traditional methods and being ready to explore new avenues.

The tools and technologies are at our disposal; it's up to us to leverage them to create a more efficient, transparent, and customer-centric real estate market.

Thank you for joining me on this journey. The future of real estate is bright, and it's driven by the power of artificial intelligence. As we move forward, let's embrace this revolution and harness its potential to build a better, more innovative industry. The future is here, and it's incredibly exciting.

www.ingramcontent.com/pod-product-compliance
Lightning Source LLC
Chambersburg PA
CBHW030452220526
45464CB00006B/2499